CULTURE, CHARACTER
& COMPENSATION

CULTURE AND CHARACTER
By R.W. EMERSON

CONTENTS

CULTURE

.

THE WORD OF AM-bition at the present day is Culture. Whilst all the world is in pursuit of power and of wealth as a means of power, cul-ture corrects the theory of success. A man is the prisoner of his power. A topical memory makes him an almanac; a talent for debate, a disputant; skill to get money makes him a miser, that is, a beggar. Culture reduces these in-flammations by invoking the aid of other powers against the dominant talent, and by appealing to the rank of powers. It watches success. For performance, Nature has no mercy, and sacrifices the performer to get it done; makes a dropsy or a tympany of him. If she wants a thumb, she makes one at the cost of arms and legs, and any excess of power in one part is usually paid for at once by some defect in a contiguous part.

Our efficiency depends so much on our con-centration, that Nature usually in the instances where a marked man is sent into the world, overloads him with bias, sacrificing his sym-metry to his working powers. It is said, no man can write but one book; and if a man

9

have a defect, it is apt to leave its impression on all his performances. If she creates a policeman like Fouché, he is made up of suspicions and of plots to circumvent them. 'The air,' said Fouché, 'is full of poniards.' The physician Sanctorius spent his life in a pair of scales, weighing his food. Lord Coke valued Chaucer highly, because the Canon Yeman's Tale illustrates the statute Hen. V. Chap. 4, against alchemy. I saw a man who believed the principal mischiefs in the English state were derived from the devotion to musical concerts. A freemason, not long since, set out to explain to this country that the principal cause of the success of General Washington was the aid he derived from the freemasons.

But worse than the harping on one string, Nature has secured individualism by giving the private person a high conceit of his weight in the system. The pest of society is egotists. There are dull and bright, sacred and profane, coarse and fine egotists. 'Tis a disease that, like influenza, falls on all constitutions. In the distemper known to physicians as chorea, the patient sometimes turns round, and continues to spin slowly on one spot. Is egotism a metaphysical varioloid of this malady? The man runs round a ring formed by his own talent, falls into an admiration of it, and loses relation to the world. It is a tendency in all minds. One of its annoying forms is a craving for sympathy. The sufferers parade their miseries, tear the lint from their bruises, reveal their indictable crimes, that you may pity them. They like sickness, because physical pain will extort some show of interest from the bystanders, as we have seen children, who, finding themselves of no account when grown people come in, will cough till they choke, to draw attention.

This distemper is the scourge of talent, of artists, inventors, and philosophers. Eminent spiritualists shall have an incapacity of putting their act or word aloof from them, and seeing it bravely for the nothing it is. Beware of the man who says, 'I am on the eve of a revelation.' It is speedily punished, inasmuch as this habit invites men to humour it, and by treating the patient tenderly, to shut him up in a narrower selfism, and exclude him from the great world of God's cheerful fallible men and women. Let us rather be insulted, whilst we are insultable. Religious literature has eminent examples, and if we run over our private list of poets, critics, philanthropists, and philosophers, we shall find them infected with this dropsy and elephantiasis, which we ought to have tapped.

This goitre of egotism is so frequent among notable persons that we must infer some strong necessity in Nature which it subserves; such as we see in the sexual attraction. The preservation of the species was a point of such necessity, that Nature has secured it at all hazards by immensely overloading the passion, at the risk of perpetual crime and disorder. So egotism has its root in the cardinal necessity by which each individual persists to be what he is.

This individuality is not only not inconsistent with culture, but is the basis of it. Every valuable nature is there in its own right, and the student we speak to must have a mother-wit invincible by his culture, which uses all books, arts, facilities, and elegances of intercourse, but is never subdued and lost in them. He only is a well-made man who has a good determination. And the end of culture is not to destroy this, God forbid! but to train away all impediment and mixture, and leave nothing but pure power. Our student must have a style and determination, and be a master of his own specialty. But, having this, he must put it behind him. He must have a catholicity, a power to see with a free and disengaged look every object. Yet is this private interest and self so overcharged, that, if a man seeks a companion who can look at objects for their own sake, and without affection or self-reference, he will find the fewest who will give him that satisfaction; whilst most men are afflicted with a coldness, an incuriosity, as soon as any object does not connect with their self-love. Though they talk of the object before them, they are thinking of themselves, and their vanity is laying little traps for your admiration.

But after a man has discovered that there are limits to the interest which his private history has for mankind, he still converses with his family, or a few companions,—perhaps with half a dozen personalities that are famous in his neighbourhood. In Boston, the question of life is the names of some eight or ten men. Have you seen Mr. Allston, Doctor Channing, Mr. Adams, Mr. Webster, Mr. Greenough? Have you heard Everett, Garrison, Father Taylor, Theodore Parker? Have you talked with Messieurs Turbinewheel, Summitlevel, and Lacofrupees? Then you may as well die. In New York, the question is of some other eight, or ten, or twenty. Have you seen a few lawyers, merchants, and brokers,—two or three scholars, two or three capitalists, two or three editors of newspapers? New York is a sucked orange. All conversation is at an end, when we have discharged ourselves of a dozen personalities, domestic or imported, which make up our American existence. Nor do we expect anybody to be other than a faint copy of these heroes.

Life is very narrow. Bring any club or company of intelligent men together again after ten years, and if the presence of some penetrating and calming genius could dispose them to frankness, what a confession of insanities would come up! The 'causes' to which we have sacrificed, Tariff or Democracy, Whiggism or Abolition, Temperance or Socialism, would show like roots of bitterness and dragons of wrath ; and our talents are as mischievous as if each had been seized upon by some bird of prey, which had whisked him away from fortune, from truth, from the dear society of the poets, some zeal, some bias, and only when he was now grey and nerveless was it relaxing its claws, and he awaking to sober perceptions.

Culture is the suggestion from certain best thoughts, that a man has a range of affinities, through which he can modulate the violence of any master-tones that have a droning preponderance in his scale, and succour him against himself. Culture redresses his balance, puts him among his equals and superiors, revives the delicious sense of sympathy, and warns him of the dangers of solitude and repulsion.

'Tis not a compliment but a disparagement to consult a man only on horses, or on steam, or on theatres, or on eating, or on books, and, whenever he appears, considerately to turn the conversation to the bantling he is known to fondle. In the Norse heaven of our forefathers, Thor's house had five hundred and forty floors; and man's house has five hundred and forty floors. His excellence is facility of adaptation and of transition through many related points, to wide contrasts and extremes. Culture kills his exaggeration, his conceit of his village or his city. We must leave our pets at home, when we go into the street, and meet men on broad grounds of good meaning and good sense. No performance is worth loss of geniality. 'Tis a cruel price we pay for certain fancy goods called fine arts and philosophy. In the Norse legend, Allfadir did not get a drink of Mimir's spring (the fountain of wisdom) until he left his eye in pledge. And here is a pedant that cannot unfold his wrinkles, nor conceal his wrath at interruption by the best, if their conversation do not fit his impertinency,—here is he to afflict us with his personalities. 'Tis incident to scholars, that each of them fancies he is pointedly odious in his community. Draw him out of this limbo of irritability. Cleanse with healthy blood his parchment skin. You restore to him his eyes which he left in pledge at Mimir's spring. If you are a victim of your doing, who cares what you do? We can spare your opera, your gazetteer, your chemic analysis, your history, your syllogisms. Your man of genius pays dear for his distinction. His head runs up into a spire, and instead of a healthy man, merry and wise, he is some mad dominie. Nature is reckless of the individual. When she has points to carry, she carries them. To wade in marshes and sea-margins is the destiny of certain birds, and they are so accurately made for this, that they are imprisoned in those places. Each animal out of its habitat would starve. To the physician, each man, each woman, is an amplification of one organ. A soldier, a locksmith, a bank-clerk, and a dancer, could not exchange functions. And thus we are victims of adaptation.

The antidotes against this organic egotism are, the range and variety of attractions, as gained by acquaintance with the world, with men of merit, with classes of society, with travel, with eminent persons, and with the high resources of philosophy, art, and religion : books, travel, society, solitude.

The hardiest sceptic who has seen a horse broken, a pointer trained, or who has visited a menagerie, or the exhibition of the Industrious Fleas, will not deny the validity of education. 'A boy,' says Plato, 'is the most vicious of all wild beasts'; and, in the same spirit, the old English poet, Gascoigne, says, 'a boy is better unborn than untaught.' The city breeds one kind of speech and manners; the back-country a different style; the sea another; the army a fourth. We know that an army which can be confided in, may be formed by discipline; that by systematic discipline all men may be made heroes: Marshal Lannes said to a French officer, 'Know, Colonel, that none but a poltroon will boast that he never was afraid.' A great part of courage is the courage of having done the thing before. And, in all human action, those faculties will be strong which are used. Robert Owen said, 'Give me a tiger, and I will educate him.' 'Tis inhuman to want faith in the power of education, since to meliorate is the law of nature; and men are valued precisely as they exert onward or meliorating force. On the other hand, poltroonery is the acknowledging an inferiority to be incurable.

Incapacity of melioration is the only mortal distemper. There are people who can never understand a trope, or any second or expanded sense given to your words, or any humour; but remain literalists, after hearing the music, and poetry, and rhetoric, and wit of seventy or eighty years. They are past the help of surgeon or clergy. But even these can understand pitchforks and the cry of fire; and I have noticed in some of this class a marked dislike of earthquakes.

Let us make our education brave and preventive. Politics is an after-work, a poor patching. We are always a little late. The evil is done, the law is passed, and we begin the uphill agitation for repeal of that of which we ought to have prevented the enacting. We shall one day learn to supersede politics by education. What we call our root-and-branch reforms of slavery, war, gambling, intemperance, is only medicating the symptoms. We must begin higher up, namely, in Education.

Our arts and tools give to him who can handle them much the same advantage over the novice as if you extended his life ten, fifty, or a hundred years. And I think it the part of good sense to provide every fine soul with such culture, that it shall not, at thirty or forty years, have to say, 'This which I might do is made hopeless through my want of weapons.'

But it is conceded that much of our training fails of effect; that all success is hazardous and rare; that a large part of our cost and pains is thrown away. Nature takes the matter into her own hands, and, though we must not omit any jot of our system, we can seldom be sure that it has availed much, or that as much good would not have accrued from a different system.

Books, as containing the finest records of human wit, must always enter into our notion of culture. The best heads that ever existed, Pericles, Plato, Julius Cæsar, Shakespeare, Goethe, Milton, were well-read, universally educated men, and quite too wise to undervalue letters. Their opinion has weight, because they had means of knowing the opposite opinion. We look that a great man should be a good reader, or, in proportion to the spontaneous power should be the assimilating power. Good criticism is very rare, and always precious. I am always happy to meet persons who perceive the transcendent superiority of Shakespeare over all other writers. I like people who like Plato. Because this love does not consist with self-conceit.

But books are good only as far as a boy is ready for them. He sometimes gets ready very slowly. You send your child to the schoolmaster, but 'tis the schoolboys who educate him. You send him to the Latin class, but much of his tuition comes, on his way to school, from the shop-windows. You like the strict rules and the long terms; and he finds his best leading in a by-way of his own, and refuses any companions but of his choosing. He hates the grammar and Gradus, and loves guns, fishing-rods, horses, and boats. Well, the boy is right; and you are not fit to direct his bringing up if your theory leaves out his gymnastic training. Archery, cricket, gun and fishing-rod, horse and boat, are all educators, liberalisers; and so are dancing, dress, and the street-talk; and,—provided only the boy has resources, and is of a noble and ingenuous strain,—these will not serve him less than the books. He learns chess, whist, dancing, and theatricals. The father observes that another boy has learned algebra and geometry in the same time. But the first boy has acquired much more than these poor games along with them. He is infatuated for weeks with whist and chess: but presently will find out, as you did, that when he rises from the game too long played he is vacant and forlorn, and despises himself. Thenceforward it takes place with other things, and has its due weight in his experience. These minor skills and accomplishments —for example, dancing—are tickets of admission to the dress-circle of mankind, and the being master of them enables the youth to judge intelligently of much on which, otherwise, he would give a pedantic squint. Landor said, ' I have suffered more from my bad dancing than from all the misfortunes and miseries of my life put together.' Provided always the boy is teachable (for we are not proposing to make a statue out of punk), football, cricket, archery, swimming, skating, climbing, fencing, riding, are lessons in the art of power, which it is his main business to learn;—riding, specially, of which Lord Herbert of Cherbury said, ' A good rider on a good horse is as much above himself and others as the world can make him.' Besides, the gun, fishing-rod, boat, and horse, constitute, among all who use them, secret freemasonries. They are as if they belonged to one club.

There is also a negative value in these arts. Their chief use to the youth is, not amusement, but to be known for what they are, and not to remain to him occasions of heartburn. We are full of superstitions. Each class fixes its eyes on the advantages it has not; the re- fined, on rude strength; the democrat, on birth and breeding. One of the benefits of a college education is, to show the boy its little avail. I knew a leading man in a leading city, who, having set his heart on an education at the university, and missed it, could never quite feel himself the equal of his own brothers who had gone thither. His easy superiority to mul- titudes of professional men could never quite countervail to him this imaginary defect. Balls, riding, wine-parties, and billiards, pass to a poor boy for something fine and romantic, which they are not; and a free admission to them on an equal footing, if it were possible, only once or twice, would be worth ten times its cost, by undeceiving him.

I am not much an advocate for travelling, and I observe that men run away to other countries because they are not good in their own, and run back to their own because they pass for nothing in the new places. For the most part, only the light characters travel. Who are you that have no task to keep you at home? I have been quoted as saying captious things about travel; but I mean to do justice. I think there is a restlessness in our people, which argues want of character. All educated Americans, first or last, go to Europe; —perhaps because it is their mental home, as the invalid habits of this country might suggest. An eminent teacher of girls said, ‘The idea of a girl's education is, whatever qualifies them for going to Europe.’ Can we never extract this tape-worm of Europe from the brain of our countrymen? One sees very well what their fate must be. He that does not fill a place at home, cannot abroad. He only goes there to hide his insignificance in a larger crowd. You do not think you will find anything there which you have not seen at home? The stuff of all countries is just the same. Do you suppose there is any country where they do not scald milkpans, and swaddle the infants, and burn the brushwood, and broil the fish? What is true anywhere is true everywhere. And let him go where he will, he can only find so much beauty or worth as he carries.

Of course, for some men, travel may be useful. Naturalists, discoverers, and sailors are born. Some men are made for couriers, exchangers, envoys, missionaries, bearers of despatches, as others are for farmers and working

23

men. And if the man is of a light and social turn, and nature has aimed to make a legged and winged creature, framed for locomotion, we must follow her hint, and furnish him with that breeding which gives currency, as sedulously as with that which gives worth. But let us not be pedantic, but allow to travel its full effect. The boy grown up on the farm, which he has never left, is said in the country to have had no chance, and boys and men of that condition look upon work on a railroad, or drudgery in a city, as opportunity. Poor country boys of Vermont and Connecticut formerly owed what knowledge they had to their peddling trips to the Southern States. California and the Pacific coast is now the university of this class, as Virginia was in old times. 'To have some chance' is their word. And the phrase, 'to know the world,' or to travel, is synonymous with all men's ideas of advantage and superiority. No doubt, to a man of sense, travel offers advantages. As many languages as he has, as many friends, as many arts and trades, so many times is he a man. A foreign country is a point of comparison wherefrom to judge his own. One use of travel is, to recommend the books and works of home [we go to Europe to be Americanised], and another, to find men. For, as nature has put fruits apart in latitudes, a new fruit in every degree, so knowledge and fine moral quality she lodges in distant men. And thus, of the six or seven teachers whom each man wants among his contemporaries, it often happens that one or two of them live on the other side of the world.

Moreover, there is in every constitution a certain solstice, when the stars stand still in our inward firmament, and when there is required some foreign force, some diversion or alterative to prevent stagnation. And, as a medical remedy, travel seems one of the best. Just as a man witnessing the admirable effect of ether to lull pain, and meditating on the contingencies of wounds, cancers, lockjaws, rejoices in Dr. Jackson's benign discovery, so a man who looks at Paris, at Naples, or at London, says, ' If I should be driven from my own home, here, at least, my thoughts can be consoled by the most prodigal amusement and occupation which the human races in ages could contrive and accumulate.'

Akin to the benefit of foreign travel, the æsthetic value of railroads is to unite the advantages of town and country life, neither of which we can spare. A man should live in or near a large town, because, let his own genius be what it may, it will repel quite as much of agreeable and valuable talent as it draws, and, in a city, the total attraction of all the citizens is sure to conquer, first or last, every repulsion, and drag the most improbable hermit within its walls some day in the year. In town, he can find the swimming school, the gymnasium, the dancing-master, the shooting-gallery, opera, theatre, and panorama; the chemist's shop, the museum of natural history; the gallery of fine arts; the national orators, in their turn; foreign travellers, the libraries, and his club. In the country he can find solitude and reading, manly labour, cheap living, and his old shoes; moors for game, hills for geology, and groves for devotion. Aubrey writes, 'I have heard Thomas Hobbes say, that, in the Earl of Devon's house, in Derbyshire, there was a good library and books enough for him, and his lordship stored the library with what books he thought fit to be bought. But the want of good conversation was a very great inconvenience, and, though he conceived he could order his thinking as well as another, yet he found a great defect. In the country, in long time, for want of good conversation, one's understanding and invention contract a moss on them, like an old paling in an orchard.'

Cities give us collision. 'Tis said London and New York take the nonsense out of a man. A great part of our education is sympathetic and social. Boys and girls who have been brought up with well-informed and superior people, show in their manners an inestimable grace. Fuller says that ' William, Earl of Nassau, won a subject from the King of Spain every time he put off his hat.' You cannot have one well-bred man without a whole society of such. They keep each other up to any high point. Especially women ;— it requires a great many cultivated women, —saloons of bright, elegant, reading women, accustomed to ease and refinement, to spectacles, pictures, sculpture, poetry, and to elegant society, in order that you should have one Madame de Staël. The head of the commercial house, or a leading lawyer or politician, is brought into daily contact with troops of men from all parts of the country, and those too the driving wheels, the business men of each section, and one can hardly suggest for an apprehensive man a more searching culture. Besides, we must remember the high social possibilities of a million of men. The best bribe which London offers to-day to the imagination is that, in such a vast variety of people and conditions, one can believe there is room for persons of romantic character to exist, and that the poet, the mystic, and the hero may hope to confront their counterparts.

I wish cities could teach their best lesson, —of quiet manners. It is the foible especially of American youth—pretension. The mark of the man of the world is absence of pretension. He does not make a speech; he takes a low business-tone, avoids all brag, is nobody, dresses plainly, promises not at all, performs much, speaks in monosyllables, hugs his fact. He calls his employment by its lowest name, and so takes from evil tongues their sharpest weapon. His conversation clings to the weather and the news, yet he allows himself to be surprised into thought, and the unlocking of his learning and philosophy. How the imagination is piqued by anecdotes of some great man passing incognito, as a king in grey clothes; of Napoleon affecting a plain suit at his glittering levee; of Burns, or Scott, or Beethoven, or Wellington, or Goethe, or any container of transcendent power, passing for nobody; of Epaminondas, 'who never says anything, but will listen eternally'; of Goethe,

who preferred trifling subjects and common ex-
pressions in intercourse with strangers, worse
rather than better clothes, and to appear a
little more capricious than he was. There are
advantages in the old hat and box-coat. I have
heard that throughout this country a certain
respect is paid to good broad-cloth ; but dress
makes a little restraint : men will not commit
themselves. But the box-coat is like wine ; it
unlocks the tongue, and men say what they
think. An old poet says :

> 'Go far and go sparing,
> For you 'll find it certain,
> The poorer and baser you appear
> The more you 'll look through still.'

Not much otherwise Milnes writes, in the Lay
of the Humble :

> ' To me men are what they are,
> They wear no masks with me.'

'Tis odd that our people should have—not
water on the brain—but a little gas there. A
shrewd foreigner said of the Americans, that,
' Whatever they say has a little the air of a
speech.' Yet one of the traits down in the
books as distinguishing the Anglo-Saxon, is,
a trick of self-disparagement. To be sure, in
old, dense countries, among a million of good
coats, a fine coat comes to be no distinction,

and you find humorists. In an English party, a man with no marked manners or features, with a face like red dough, unexpectedly discloses wit, learning, a wide range of topics, and personal familiarity with good men in all parts of the world, until you think you have fallen upon some illustrious personage. Can it be that the American forest has refreshed some weeds of old Pictish barbarism just ready to die out,—the love of the scarlet feather, of beads, and tinsel? The Italians are fond of red clothes, peacock plumes, and embroidery; and I remember one rainy morning in the city of Palermo, the street was in a blaze with scarlet umbrellas. The English have a plain taste. The equipages of the grandees are plain. A gorgeous livery indicates new and awkward city wealth. Mr. Pitt, like Mr. Pym, thought the title of Mister good against any king in Europe. They have piqued themselves on governing the whole world in the poor, plain, dark Committee-room which the House of Commons sat in before the fire.

Whilst we want cities as the centres where the best things are found, cities degrade us by magnifying trifles. The countryman finds the town a chop-house, a barber's shop. He has lost the lines of grandeur of the horizon, hills and plains, and with them sobriety and eleva- tion. He has come among a supple, glib-tongued tribe, who live for show, servile to public opinion. Life is dragged down to a fracas of pitiful cares and disasters. You say the gods ought to respect a life whose objects are their own; but in cities they have betrayed you to a cloud of insignificant annoyances:

> 'Mirmidons, race féconde,
> Mirmidons,
> Enfin nous commandons;
> Jupiter livre le monde
> Aux mirmidons, aux mirmidons.'

> ''Tis heavy odds
> Against the gods,
> When they will match with myrmidons.
> We spawning, spawning myrmidons,
> Our turn to-day! we take command,
> Jove gives the globe into the hand
> Of myrmidons, of myrmidons.'

What is odious but noise, and people who scream and bewail? people whose vane points always east, who live to dine, who send for the doctor, who coddle themselves, who toast their feet on the register, who intrigue to secure a padded chair, and a corner out of the draught? Suffer them once to begin the enumeration of their infirmities, and the sun will go down on

the unfinished tale. Let these triflers put us
out of conceit with petty comforts. To a man
at work, the frost is but a colour: the rain, the
wind, he forgot them when he came in. Let
us learn to live coarsely, dress plainly, and lie
hard. The least habit of dominion over the
palate has certain good effects not easily esti-
mated. Neither will we be driven into a quid-
dling abstemiousness. 'Tis a superstition to
insist on a special diet. All is made at last of
the same chemical atoms.

A man in pursuit of greatness feels no little
wants. How can you mend diet, bed, dress,
or salutes or compliments, or the figure you
make in company, or wealth, or even the bringing things to pass, when you think how paltry
are the machinery and the workers? Wordsworth was praised to me, in Westmoreland, for
having afforded to his country neighbours an
example of a modest household where com-
fort and culture were secured, without display.
And a tender boy who wears his rusty cap and
out-grown coat, that he may secure the coveted
place in college, and the right in the library, is
educated to some purpose. There is a great
deal of self-denial and manliness in poor and
middle-class houses, in town, and country, that
has not got into literature, and never will, but

that keeps the earth sweet; that saves on superfluities, and spends on essentials; that goes rusty, and educates the boy; that sells the horse, but builds the school; works early and late, takes two looms in the factory, three looms, six looms, but pays off the mortgage on the paternal farm, and then goes back cheerfully to work again.

We can ill spare the commanding social benefits of cities; they must be used; yet cautiously, and haughtily,—and will yield their best values to him who best can do without them. Keep the town for occasions, but the habits should be formed to retirement. Solitude, the safeguard of mediocrity, is to genius the stern friend, the cold, obscure shelter where moult the wings which will bear it farther than suns and stars. He who should inspire and lead his race must be defended from travelling with the souls of other men, from living, breathing, reading, and writing in the daily, time-worn yoke of their opinions. 'In the morning, solitude,' said Pythagoras; that nature may speak to the imagination, as she does never in company, and that her favourite may make acquaintance with those divine strengths which disclose themselves to serious and abstracted thought. 'Tis very certain that Plato

c　　33

Plotinus, Archimedes, Hermes, Newton, Milton, Wordsworth, did not live in a crowd, but descended into it from time to time as benefactors: and the wise instructor will press this point of securing to the young soul in the disposition of time and the arrangements of living, periods and habits of solitude. The high advantage of university life is often the mere mechanical one, I may call it, of a separate chamber and fire,—which parents will allow the boy without hesitation at Cambridge, but do not think needful at home. We say solitude, to mark the character of the tone of thought; but if it can be shared between two or more than two, it is happier, and not less noble. 'We four,' wrote Neander to his sacred friends, 'will enjoy at Halle the inward blessedness of a civitas Dei, whose foundations are for ever friendship. The more I know of you, the more I dissatisfy and must dissatisfy all my wonted companions. Their very presence stupefies me. The common understanding withdraws itself from the one centre of all existence.'

Solitude takes off the pressure of present importunities that more catholic and humane relations may appear. The saint and poet seek privacy to ends the most public and universal:

34

and it is the secret of culture to interest the man more in his public than in his private quality. Here is a new poem, which elicits a good many comments in the journals, and in conversation. From these it is easy, at last, to eliminate the verdict which readers passed upon it; and that is, in the main, unfavourable. The poet, as a craftsman, is only interested in the praise accorded to him, and not in the censure, though it be just. And the poor little poet hearkens only to that, and rejects the censure, as proving incapacity in the critic. But the poet cultivated becomes a stockholder in both companies,—say Mr. Curfew,—in the Curfew stock, and in the humanity stock; and, in the last, exults as much in the demonstration of the unsoundness of Curfew, as his interest in the former gives him pleasure in the currency of Curfew. For, the depreciation of his Curfew stock only shows the immense values of the humanity stock. As soon as he sides with his critic against himself, with joy, he is a cultivated man.

We must have an intellectual quality in all property and in all action, or they are nought. I must have children, I must have events, I must have a social state and history, or my thinking and speaking want body or basis. But to give these accessories any value, I must know them as contingent and rather showy possessions, which pass for more to the people than to me. We see this abstraction in scholars as a matter of course: but what a charm it adds when observed in practical men. Bonaparte, like Cæsar, was intellectual, and could look at every object for itself, without affection. Though an egotist à l'outrance, he could criticise a play, a building, a character, on universal grounds, and give a just opinion. A man known to us only as a celebrity in politics or in trade, gains largely in our esteem if we discover that he has some intellectual taste or skill; as when we learn of Lord Fairfax, the Long Parliament's general, his passion for antiquarian studies; or of the French regicide Carnot, his sublime genius in mathematics; or of a living banker, his success in poetry; or of a partisan journalist, his devotion to ornithology. So, if in travelling in the dreary wilderness of Arkansas or Texas, we should observe on the next seat a man reading Horace, or Martial, or Calderon, we should wish to hug him. In callings that require roughest energy, soldiers, sea-captains, and civil engineers sometimes betray a fine insight, if only through a certain gentleness when off duty; a good-natured admission that there are illusions, and who shall say that he is not their sport? We only vary the phrase, not the doctrine, when we say, that culture opens the sense of beauty. A man is a beggar who only lives to the useful, and, however he may serve as a pin or rivet in the social machine, cannot be said to have arrived at self-possession. I suffer, every day, from the want of perception of beauty in people. They do not know the charm with which all moments and objects can be embellished, the charm of manners, of self-command, of benevolence. Repose and cheerfulness are the badge of the gentleman,—repose in energy. The Greek battle-pieces are calm; the heroes, in whatever violent actions engaged, retain a serene aspect; as we say of Niagara, that it falls without speed. A cheerful, intelligent face is the end of culture, and success enough. For it indicates the purpose of nature and wisdom attained.

When our higher faculties are in activity, we are domesticated, and awkwardness and discomfort give place to natural and agreeable movements. It is noticed, that the consideration of the great periods and spaces of

astronomy induces a dignity of mind, and an
indifference to death.   The influence of fine
scenery, the presence of mountains, appeases
our irritations and elevates our friendships.
Even a high dome, and the expansive exterior
of a cathedral, have a sensible effect on manners.   I have heard that stiff people lose
something of their awkwardness under high
ceilings, and in spacious halls. I think sculpture and painting have an effect to teach us
manners and abolish hurry.

But, over all, culture must reinforce from
higher influx the empirical skills of eloquence,
or of politics, or of trade, and the useful arts.
There is a certain loftiness of thought and
power to marshal and adjust particulars, which
can only come from an insight of their whole
connection.   The orator who has once seen
things in their divine order, will never quite
lose sight of this, and will come to affairs as
from a higher ground, and, though he will say
nothing of philosophy, he will have a certain
mastery in dealing with them, and an incap-
ableness of being dazzled or frighted, which
will distinguish his handling from that of at-
torneys and factors.   A man who stands on
a good footing with the heads of parties at
Washington, reads the rumours of the news-

38

papers, and the guesses of provincial politicians with a key to the right and wrong in each statement, and sees well enough where all this will end. Archimedes will look through your Connecticut machine, at a glance, and judge of its fitness. And much more, a wise man who knows not only what Plato, but what Saint John, can show him, can easily raise the affair he deals with to a certain majesty. Plato says, Pericles owed this elevation to the lessons of Anaxagoras. Burke descended from a higher sphere when he would influence human affairs. Franklin, Adams, Jefferson, Washington, stood on a fine humanity, before which the brawls of modern senates are but pot-house politics.

But there are higher secrets of culture, which are not for the apprentices, but for proficients. These are lessons only for the brave. We must know our friends under ugly masks. The calamities are our friends. Ben Jonson specifies in his address to the Muse:

' Get him the time's long grudge, the court's
      ill-will,
And, reconciled, keep him suspected still,
Make him lose all his friends, and, what is
      worse,
Almost all ways to any better course;

39

With me thou leav'st a better Muse than
thee,
And which thou brought'st me, blessed
Poverty.'
We wish to learn philosophy by rote, and play
at heroism. But the wiser God says, Take the
shame, the poverty, and the penal solitude,
that belong to truth-speaking. Try the rough
water as well as the smooth. Rough water can
teach lessons worth knowing. When the state
is unquiet, personal qualities are more than
ever decisive. Fear not a revolution which
will constrain you to live five years in one.
Don't be so tender at making an enemy now
and then. Be willing to go to Coventry sometimes, and let the populace bestow on you
their coldest contempts. The finished man of
the world must eat of every apple once. He
must hold his hatreds also at arm's length, and
not remember spite. He has neither friends
nor enemies, but values men only as channels
of power.

He who aims high, must dread an easy home
and popular manners. Heaven sometimes
hedges a rare character about with ungainli-
ness and odium, as the burr that protects the
fruit. If there is any great and good thing in
store for you, it will not come at the first or

the second call, nor in the shape of fashion, ease, and city drawing-rooms. Popularity is for dolls. 'Steep and craggy,' said Porphyry, 'is the path of the gods.' Open your Marcus Antoninus. In the opinion of the ancients, he was the great man who scorned to shine, and who contested the frowns of fortune. They preferred the noble vessel too late for the tide, contending with winds and waves, dismantled and unrigged, to her companion borne into harbour with colours flying and guns firing. There is none of the social goods that may not be purchased too dear, and mere amiableness must not take rank with high aims and self-subsistency.

Bettine replies to Goethe's mother, who chides her disregard of dress,—'If I cannot do as I have a mind, in our poor Frankfort, I shall not carry things far.' And the youth must rate at its true mark the inconceivable levity of local opinion. The longer we live, the more we must endure the elementary existence of men and women; and every brave heart must treat society as a child, and never allow it to dictate.

'All that class of the severe and restrictive virtues,' said Burke, 'are almost too costly for humanity.' Who wishes to be severe? Who wishes to resist the eminent and polite, in behalf

of the poor, and low, and impolite? and who that
dares do it can keep his temper sweet, his frolic
spirits? The high virtues are not debonair, but
have their redress in being illustrious at last.
What forests of laurel we bring, and the tears
of mankind, to those who stood firm against
the opinion of their contemporaries! The
measure of a master is his success in bringing
all men round to his opinion twenty years later.

Let me say here, that culture cannot begin
too early. In talking with scholars, I observe
that they lost on ruder companions those years
of boyhood which alone could give imaginative
literature a religious and infinite quality in their
esteem. I find, too, that the chance for appre-
ciation is much increased by being the son of
an appreciator, and that these boys who now
grow up are caught not only years too late, but
two or three births too late, to make the best
scholars of. And I think it a presentable motive
to a scholar that as, in an old community, a well-
born proprietor is usually found, after the first
heats of youth, to be a careful husband, and to
feel a habitual desire that the state shall suffer
no harm by his administration, but shall be de-
livered down to the next heir in as good condition as he received it;—so, a considerate man
will reckon himself a subject of that secular

melioration by which mankind is mollified, Let the new creature emerge erect and free cured, and refined, and will shun every expenditure of his forces on pleasure or gain, which will jeopardise this social and secular accumulation.

The fossil strata show us that nature began with rudimental forms, and rose to the more complex, as fast as the earth was fit for their dwelling-place ; and that the lower perish, as the higher appear. Very few of our race can be said to be yet finished men. We still carry sticking to us some remains of the preceding inferior quadruped organisation. We call these millions men; but they are not yet men. Half-engaged in the soil, pawing to get free, man needs all the music that can be brought to disengage him. If Love, red Love, with tears and joy; if Want with his scourge; if War with his cannonade; if Christianity with its charity; if Trade with its money ; if Art with its portfolios; if Science with her telegraphs through the deeps of space and time—can set his dull nerves throbbing, and, by loud taps on the tough .chrysalis, can break its walls, and let the new creature emerge erect and free,—make way, and sing pæan ! The age of the quadruped is to go out,—the age of the brain and of the heart is to come in. The time will come when the

Nothing he will not overcome and convert evil forms we have known can no more be organised. Man's culture can spare nothing, wants all the material. He is to convert all impediments into instruments, all enemies into power. The formidable mischief will only make the more useful slave. And if one shall read the future of the race hinted in the organic effort of nature to mount and meliorate, and the corresponding impulse to the better in the human being, we shall dare affirm that there is nothing he will not overcome and convert, until at last culture shall absorb the chaos and gehenna. He will convert the Furies into Muses, and the hells into benefit.

CHARACTER

The sun set ; but set not his hope :
Stars rose ; his faith was earlier up :
Fixed on the enormous galaxy,
Deeper and older seemed his eye :
And matched his sufferance sublime
The taciturnity of time.
He spoke, and words more soft than rain
Brought the Age of Gold again :
His action won such reverence sweet
As hid all measure of the feat.

Work of his hand
He nor commends nor grieves :
Pleads for itself the fact ;
As unrepenting Nature leaves
Her every act.

I HAVE READ THAT those who listened to Lord Chatham felt that there was something finer in the man, than anything which he said. It has been complained of our brilliant English historian of the French Revolution, that when he has told all his facts about Mirabeau, they do not justify his estimate of his genius. The Gracchi, Agis, Cleomenes, and others of Plutarch's heroes, do not in the record of facts equal their own fame. Sir Philip Sidney, the Earl of Essex, Sir Walter Raleigh are men of great figure and of few deeds. We cannot find the smallest part of the personal weight of Washington in the narrative of his exploits. The authority of the name of Schiller is too great for his books. This inequality of the reputation to the works or the anecdotes, is not accounted for by saying that the reverberation is longer than the thunder-clap; but somewhat resided in these men which begot an expectation that outran all their performance. The largest part of their power was latent. This is that which we call Character,—a reserved force which acts directly by presence, and without means.

47

It is conceived of as a certain undemonstrable force, a Familiar or Genius, by whose impulses the man is guided, but whose counsels he cannot impart; which is company for him, so that such men are often solitary, or if they chance to be social, do not need society, but can entertain themselves very well alone. The purest literary talent appears at one time great, at another small, but character is of a stellar and undiminishable greatness. What others effect by talent or by eloquence, this man accomplishes by some magnetism. 'Half his strength he put not forth.' His victories are by demonstration of superiority, and not by crossing of bayonets. He conquers, because his arrival alters the face of affairs. ' "O Iole! how did you know that Hercules was a god?" "Because," answered Iole, "I was content the moment my eyes fell on him. When I beheld Theseus, I desired that I might see him offer battle, or at least guide his horses in the chariot race: but Hercules did not wait for a contest; he conquered whether he stood, or walked, or sat, or whatever thing he did."' Man, ordinarily a pendant to events, only half attached, and that awkwardly, to the world he lives in, in these examples appears to share the life of things, and to be an expression of the same

laws which control the tides and the sun,
numbers and quantities.

In our political elections, where this element, if it appears at all, can only occur in its coarsest form, we sufficiently understand its incomparable rate. The people know that they need in their representative much more than talent, namely, the power to make his talent trusted. They cannot come at their ends by sending to Congress a learned, acute, and fluent speaker, if he be not one who, before he was appointed by the people to represent them, was appointed by Almighty God to stand for a fact,—invincibly persuaded of that fact in himself,—so that the most confident and the most violent persons learn that here is resistance on which both impudence and terror are wasted, namely, faith in a fact. The men who carry their points do not need to inquire of their constituents what they should say, but are themselves the country which they represent: nowhere are its emotions or opinions so instant and true as in them; nowhere so pure from a selfish infusion. The constituency at home hearkens to their words, watches the colour of their cheek, and therein, as in a glass, dresses its own. Our public assemblies are pretty good tests of manly force. Our frank countrymen of the west and south have a taste for character, and like to know whether the New Englander is a substantial man, or whether the hand can pass through him.

The same motive force appears in trade. There are geniuses in trade, as well as in war, or the state, or letters; and the reason why this or that man is fortunate, is not to be told. It lies in the man; that is all anybody can tell you about it. See him, and you will know as easily why he succeeds, as, if you see Napoleon, you would comprehend his fortune. In the new objects we recognise the old game, the habit of fronting the fact, and not dealing with it at second hand, through the perceptions of somebody else. Nature herself seems to authorise trade, as soon as you see the natural merchant, who appears not so much a private agent, as her factor and Minister of Commerce. His natural probity combines with his insight into the fabric of society, to put him above tricks, and he communicates to all his own faith, that contracts are of no private interpretation. The habit of his mind is a reference to standards of natural equity and public advantage; and he inspires respect, and the wish to deal with him, both for the quiet spirit of honour which attends him, and for the intellectual pastime

which the spectacle of so much ability affords. Being an agent of original laws
This immensely stretched trade, which makes
the Capes of the Southern Ocean his wharfs,
and the Atlantic Sea his familiar port, centres
in his brain only: and nobody in the universe
can make his place good. In his parlour, I
see very well that he has been at hard work
this morning, with that knitted brow, and that
settled humour, which all his desire to be
courteous cannot shake off. I see plainly how
many firm acts have been done; how many
valiant noes have this day been spoken, when
others would have uttered ruinous yeas. I
see, with the pride of art, and skill of masterly
arithmetic and power of remote combination,
his consciousness of being an agent and play-
fellow of the original laws of the world. He
too believes that none can supply him, and that
a man must be born to trade, or he cannot
learn it.

This virtue draws the mind more, when it
appears in action, to ends not so mixed. It
works with most energy in the smallest companies and in private relations. In all cases,
it is an extraordinary and incomputable agent.
The excess of physical strength is paralysed by
it. Higher natures overpower lower ones by
affecting them with a certain sleep. The facul-

ties are locked up, and offer no resistance. Perhaps that is the universal law. When the high
cannot bring up the low to itself, it benumbs
it, as man charms down the resistance of the
lower animals. Men exert on each other a
similar occult power. How often has the influence of a true master realised all the tales
of magic! A river of command seemed to run
down from his eyes into all those who beheld
him, a torrent of strong sad light, like an Ohio
or Danube, which pervaded them with his
thoughts, and coloured all events with the hue
of his mind. 'What means did you employ?'
was the question asked of the wife of Concini,
in regard to her treatment of Mary of Medici;
and the answer was, 'Only that influence which
every strong mind has over a weak one.' Cannot Cæsar in irons shuffle off the irons, and
transfer them to the person of Hippo or Thraso
the turnkey? Is an iron handcuff so immut-
able a bond? Suppose a slaver on the coast
of Guinea should take on board a gang of
negroes, which should contain persons of the
stamp of Toussaint L'Ouverture: or, let us
fancy, under these swarthy masks he has a
gang of Washingtons in chains. When they
arrive at Cuba, will the relative order of the
ship's company be the same? Is there nothing

but rope and iron? Is there no love, no rever- ence? Is there never a glimpse of right in a poor slave-captain's mind; and cannot these be supposed available to break, or elude, or in any manner overmatch the tension of an inch or two of iron ring?

Character is a natural power, like light and heat, and all nature co-operates with it. The reason why we feel one man's presence, and do not feel another's, is as simple as gravity. Truth is the summit of being· justice is the application of it to affairs. All individual natures stand in a scale, according to the purity of this element in them. The will of the pure runs down from them into other natures, as water runs down from a higher into a lower vessel. This natural force is no more to be withstood, than any other natural force. We can drive a stone upward for a moment into the air, but it is yet true that all stones will for ever fall; and whatever instances can be quoted of unpunished theft, or of a lie which somebody credited, justice must prevail, and it is the privilege of truth to make itself believed. Character is this moral order seen through the medium of an individual nature. An individual is an encloser. Time and space, liberty and necessity, truth and thought, are left at large no

53

longer. Now, the universe is a close or pound.
All things exist in the man tinged with the
manners of his soul. With what quality is in
him, he infuses all nature that he can reach;
nor does he tend to lose himself in vastness,
but, how long a curve soever, all his regards
return into his own good at last. He animates
all he can, and he sees only what he animates.
He encloses the world, as the patriot does his
country, as a material basis for his character,
and a theatre for action. A healthy soul stands
united with the Just and the True, as the
magnet arranges itself with the pole, so that
he stands to all beholders like a transparent
object betwixt them and the sun, and whoso
journeys towards the sun, journeys towards
that person. He is thus the medium of the
highest influence to all who are not on the same
level. Thus, men of character are the con-
science of the society to which they belong.

The natural measure of this power is the resistance of circumstances. Impure men consider life as it is reflected in opinions, events,
and persons. They cannot see the action, until
it is done. Yet its moral element pre-existed
in the actor, and its quality as right or wrong,
it was easy to predict. Everything in nature
is bipolar, or has a positive and negative pole.

There is a male and a female, a spirit and a fact, a north and a south. Spirit is the positive, the event is the negative. Will is the north, action the south pole. Character may be ranked as having its natural place in the north. It shares the magnetic currents of the system. The feeble souls are drawn to the south or negative pole. They look at the profit or hurt of the action. They never behold a principle until it is lodged in a person. They do not wish to be lovely, but to be loved. One class of character like to hear of their faults: the other class do not like to hear of their faults; they worship events; secure to them a fact, a connexion, a certain chain of circumstances, and they will ask no more. The hero sees that the event is ancillary: it must follow him. A given order of events has no power to secure to him the satisfaction which the imagination attaches to it; the soul of goodness escapes from any set of circumstances, whilst prosperity belongs to a certain mind, and will introduce that power and victory which is its natural fruit, into any order of events. No change of circumstances can repair a defect of character. We boast our emancipation from many superstitions; but if we have broken any idols, it is through a transfer of the idolatry.

What have I gained, that I no longer immolate a bull to Jove, or to Neptune, or a mouse to Hecate; that I do not tremble before the Eumenides, or the Catholic Purgatory, or the Calvinistic Judgment-day,—if I quake at opinion, the public opinion, as we call it; or at the threat of assault, or contumely, or bad neighbours, or poverty, or mutilation, or at the rumour of revolution, or of murder? If I quake, what matters it what I quake at? Our proper vice takes form in one or another shape, according to the sex, age, or temperament of the person, and, if we are capable of fear, will readily find terrors. The covetousness or the malignity which saddens me, when I ascribe it to society, is my own. I am always environed by myself. On the other part, rectitude is a perpetual victory, celebrated not by cries of joy, but by serenity, which is joy fixed or habitual. It is disgraceful to fly to events for confirmation of our truth and worth. The capitalist does not run every hour to the broker, to coin his advantages into current money of the realm; he is satisfied to read in the quotations of the market, that his stocks have risen. The same transport which the occurrence of the best events in the best order would occasion me, I must learn to taste purer in the perception that my position is every hour meliorated, and does already command those events I desire. The exultation is only to be checked by the foresight of an order of things so excellent, as to throw all our prosperities into the deepest shade.

The face which character wears to me is self-sufficingness. I revere the person who has riches; so that I cannot think of him as alone, or poor, or exiled, or unhappy, or a client, but as perpetual patron, benefactor, and beatified man. Character is centrality, the impossibility of being displaced or overset. A man should give us a sense of mass. Society is frivolous, and shreds its day into scraps, its conversation into ceremonies and escapes. But if I go to see an ingenious man, I shall think myself poorly entertained if he give me nimble pieces of benevolence and etiquette; rather he shall stand stoutly in his place, and let me apprehend, if it were only his resistance, and know that I have encountered a new and positive quality; —great refreshment for both of us. It is much that he does not accept the conventional opinions and practices. His nonconformity will remain a goad and a remembrancer, and every inquirer will have to dispose of him, in the first place. There is nothing real or useful

that is not a seat of war. Our houses ring with
laughter and personal and critical gossip, but
it helps little. The uncivil, unavailable man,
who is a problem and a threat to society, whom
it cannot let pass in silence, but must either
worship or hate,—and to whom all parties feel
related, both the leaders of opinion, and the
obscure and eccentric,—he helps; he puts
America and Europe in the wrong, and de-
stroys the scepticism which says, 'man is a doll,
let us eat and drink, 'tis the best we can do,'
by drawing attention to the untried and unknown. Acquiescence in the establishment,
and appeal to the public, indicate infirm faith,
heads which are not clear, and which must see
a house built, before they can comprehend the
plan of it. The wise man not only leaves out
of his thought the many, but leaves out the
few. Fountains, the self-moved, the absorbed,
the commander because he is commanded,
the assured, the primary,—they are good; for
these announce the instant presence of supreme power.

Our action should rest mathematically on
our substance. In nature, there are no false
valuations. A pound of water in the ocean-
tempest has no more gravity than in a mid-
summer pond. All things work exactly ac-

cording to their quality, and according to their quantity; attempt nothing they cannot do; except man only: he has pretension: he wishes and attempts things beyond his force. I read in a book of English memoirs, 'Mr. Fox (afterwards Lord Holland) said, he must have the Treasury; he had served up to it, and would have it.'—Xenophon and his Ten Thousand were quite equal to what they attempted, and did it; so equal, that it was not suspected to be a grand and inimitable exploit. Yet there stands that fact unrepeated, a high-water mark in military history. Many have attempted it since, and not been equal to it. It is only on reality, that any power of action can be based. No institution will be better than the institutor. I knew an amiable and accomplished person who undertook a practical reform, yet I was never able to find in him the enterprise of love he took in hand. He adopted it by ear and by the understanding, from the books he had been reading. All his action was tentative, a piece of the city carried out into the fields, and was the city still, and no new fact, and could not inspire enthusiasm. Had there been something latent in the man, a terrible undemonstrated genius agitating and embarrassing his demeanour, we had watched for its advent. It

59

is not enough that the intellect should see the evils, and their remedy. We shall still postpone our existence, nor take the ground to which we are entitled, whilst it is only a thought, and not a spirit that incites us. We have not yet served up to it.

These are properties of life, and another trait is the notice of incessant growth. Men should be intelligent and earnest; they must also make us feel, that they have a controlling happy future, opening before them, which sheds a splendour on the passing hour. The hero is misconceived and misreported: he cannot therefore wait to unravel any man's blunders: he is again on the road, adding new powers and honours to his domain, and new claims on your heart, which will bankrupt you, if you have loitered about the old things, and have not kept your relation to him, by adding to your wealth. New actions are the only apologies and explanations of old ones, which the noble can bear to offer or to receive. If your friend has displeased you, you shall not sit down to consider it, for he has already lost all memory of the passage, and has doubled his power to serve you, and, ere you can rise up again, will burden you with blessings.

We have no pleasure in thinking of a benevolence that is only measured by its works. Those who live to the future must appear selfish Love is inexhaustible, and if its estate is wasted, its granary emptied, still cheers and enriches, and the man, though he sleep, seems to purify the air, and his house to adorn the landscape and strengthen the laws. People always recognise this difference. We know who is benevolent, by quite other means than the amount of subscription to soup-societies. It is only low merits that can be enumerated. Fear, when your friends say to you what you have done well, and say it through ; but when they stand with uncertain timid looks of respect and half-dislike, and must suspend their judgment for years to come, you may begin to hope. Those who live to the future must always appear selfish to those who live to the present. It was droll in the good Riemer, who has written memoirs of Goethe, to make out a list of his donations and good deeds : as, so many hundred thalers given to Stilling, to Hegel, to Tischbein ; a lucrative place found for Professor Voss, a post under the Grand Duke for Herder, a pension for Meyer, two professors recommended to foreign universities, etc. etc. The longest list of specifications of benefit would look very short. A man is a poor creature, if he is to be measured so. For, all these, of course, are exceptions; and the rule and hodiernal life of a good man is benefaction. The true charity of Goethe is to be inferred from the account he gave Dr. Eckermann, of the way in which he spent his fortune. ' Each bonmot of mine has cost a purse of gold. Half a million of my own money, the fortune I inherited, my salary, and the large income derived from my writings for fifty years back, have been expended to instruct me in what I now know. I have besides seen, etc.'

It is but poor chat and gossip to go to enumerate traits of this simple and rapid power, and we are painting the lightning with charcoal; but in these long nights and vacations, we like to console ourselves so. Nothing but itself can copy it. A word warm from the heart enriches me. I surrender at discretion. How death-cold is literary genius before this fire of life! These are the touches that reanimate my heavy soul, and give it eyes to pierce the dark of nature. I find, where I thought myself poor, there I was most rich. Thence comes a new intellectual exaltation, to be again rebuked by some new exhibition of character. Strange alternation of attraction and repulsion! Character repudiates intellect, yet excites it; and character passes into thought, is published so, and then is ashamed before new flashes of moral worth.

Character is nature in the highest form. It is of no use to ape it, or to contend with it. Somewhat is possible of resistance, and of persistence, and of creation, to this power, which will foil all emulation.

This masterpiece is best where no hands but nature's have been laid on it. Care is taken that the greatly-destined shall slip up into life in the shade, with no thousand-eyed Athens to watch and blazon every new thought, every blushing emotion of young genius. Two persons lately,—very young children of the most high God,—have given me occasion for thought. When I explored the source of their sanctity, and charm for the imagination, it seemed as if each answered, ' From my nonconformity : I never listened to your people's law, or to what they call their gospel, and wasted my time. I was content with the simple rural poverty of my own : hence this sweetness : my work never reminds you of that ;— is pure of that.' And nature advertises me in such persons, that, in democratic America, she will not be democratised. How cloistered and constitutionally sequestered from the market and from scandal ! It was only this morning

that I sent away some records, which were wild
flowers of these wood-gods. They are a relief
from literature,—these fresh draughts from the
sources of thought and sentiment; as we read,
in an age of polish and criticism, the first lines
of written prose and verse of a nation. How
captivating is their devotion to their favourite books, whether Æschylus, Dante, Shakespeare, or Scott, as feeling that they have a stake
in that book: who touches that, touches them;
—and especially the total solitude of the critic,
the Patmos of thought from which he writes,
in unconsciousness of any eyes that shall ever
read this writing. Could they dream on still,
as angels, and not wake to comparisons, and
to be flattered! Yet some natures are too good
to be spoiled by praise; and wherever the vein
of thought reaches down into the profound,
there is no danger from vanity. Solemn friends
will warn them of the danger of their heads
being turned by the flourish of trumpets, but
they can afford to smile. I remember the indignation of an eloquent Methodist at the kind
admonition of a Doctor of Divinity: 'My friend,
a man can neither be praised nor insulted.' But
forgive the counsels; they are very natural. I
remember the thought which occurred to me
when some ingenious and spiritual foreigners

came to America, was, 'Have you been victim-
ised in being brought hither?'—or, prior to Those saluted as divine
that, answer me this : ' Are you victimisable?'

As I have said, nature keeps these sove-
reignties in her own hands, and however pertly
our sermons and disciplines would divide some
share of credit, and teach that the laws fashion
the citizen, she goes her own gait, and puts
the wisest in the wrong. She makes very light
of gospels and prophets, as one who has a great
many more to produce, and no excess of time
to spare on any one. There is a class of men,
individuals of which appear at long intervals,
so eminently endowed with insight and virtue,
that they have been unanimously saluted as
divine, and who seem to be an accumulation
of that power we consider. Divine persons are
character born, or, to borrow a phrase from
Napoleon, they are victory organised. They
are usually received with ill-will, because they
are new, and because they set a bound to the
exaggeration that has been made of the per-
sonality of the last divine person. Nature
never rhymes her children, nor makes two men
alike. When we see a great man, we fancy a
resemblance to some historical person, and
predict the sequel of his character and fortune,
a result which he is sure to disappoint. None

E   65

will ever solve the problem of his character according to our prejudice, but only in his own unprecedented way. Character wants room; must not be crowded on by persons, nor be judged from glimpses got in the press of affairs or on few occasions. It needs perspective, as a great building. It may not, probably does not, form relationships rapidly: and we should not require rash explanation, either on the popular ethics, or on our own, of its action.

I look on Sculpture as history. I do not think the Apollo and the Jove impossible in flesh and blood. Every trait which the artist recorded in stone he had seen in life, and better than his copy. We have seen many counterfeits, but we are born believers in great men. How easily we read in old books, when men were few, of the smallest action of the patriarchs. We require that a man should be so large and columnar in the landscape, that it should deserve to be recorded, that he arose and girded up his loins, and departed to such a place. The pictures most credible to us are those of majestic men who prevailed at their entrance, and convinced the senses; as happened to the eastern magian who was sent to test the merits of Zertusht or Zoroaster.

When the Yunani sage arrived at Balkh, the Persians tell us, Gushtasp appointed a day on which the Mobeds of every country should assemble, and a golden chair was placed for the Yunani sage. Then the beloved Yezdam, the prophet Zertusht, advanced into the midst of the assembly. The Yunani sage, on seeing that chief, said, ' This form and this gait cannot lie, and nothing but truth can proceed from them.' Plato said, it was impossible not to believe in the children of the gods, ' though they should speak without probable or necessary arguments.' I should think myself very unhappy in my associates, if I could not credit the best things in history. ' John Bradshaw,' says Milton, 'appears like a consul, from whom the fasces are not to depart with the year; so that not on the tribunal only, but throughout his life, you would regard him as sitting in judgment upon kings.' I find it more credible, since it is anterior information, that one man should know heaven, as the Chinese say, than that so many men should know the world. ' The virtuous prince confronts the gods, without any misgiving. He waits a hundred ages till a sage comes and does not doubt. He who confronts the gods, without any misgiving, knows heaven; he who waits a hundred ages

until a sage comes without doubting, knows
men. Hence the virtuous prince moves, and
for ages shows empire the way.' But there is
no need to seek remote examples. He is a dull
observer whose experience has not taught him
the reality and force of magic, as well as of
chemistry. The coldest precisian cannot go
abroad without encountering inexplicable influences. One man fastens an eye on him, and
the graves of the memory render up their dead;
the secrets that make him wretched either to
keep or to betray, must be yielded;—another,
and he cannot speak, and the bones of his body
seem to lose their cartilages; the entrance of a
friend adds grace, boldness, and eloquence to
him; and there are persons, he cannot choose
but remember, who gave a transcendent expansion to his thought, and kindled another
life in his bosom.

What is so excellent as strict relations of
amity, when they spring from this deep root?
The sufficient reply to the sceptic, who doubts
the power and the furniture of man, is in that
possibility of joyful intercourse with persons,
which makes the faith and practice of all rea-
sonable men. I know nothing which life has
to offer so satisfying as the profound good
understanding, which can subsist, after much

exchange of good offices, between two virtu- ous men, each of whom is sure of himself, and sure of his friend. It is a happiness which postpones all other gratifications, and makes politics, and commerce, and churches, cheap. For, when men shall meet as they ought, each a benefactor, a shower of stars, clothed with thoughts, with deeds, with accomplishments, it should be the festival of nature which all things announce. Of such friendship, love in the sexes is the first symbol, as all other things are symbols of love. Those relations to the best men, which, at one time, we reckoned the romances of youth, become, in the progress of the character, the most solid enjoyment.

If it were possible to live in right relations with men!—if we could abstain from asking anything of them, from asking their praise, or help, or pity, and content us with compelling them through the virtue of the eldest laws! could we not deal with a few persons—with one person—after the unwritten statutes, and make an experiment of their efficacy? Could we not pay our friend the compliment of truth, of silence, of forbearing? Need we be so eager to seek him? If we are related, we shall meet. It was a tradition of the ancient world, that no metamorphosis could hide a god from a god; and there is a Greek verse which runs,

'The gods are to each other not unknown.'
Friends also follow the laws of divine necessity; they gravitate to each other, and cannot otherwise :—

'When each the other shall avoid,
Shall each by each be most enjoyed.'

Their relation is not made, but allowed. The gods must seat themselves without seneschal in our Olympus, and as they can instal themselves by divine seniority. Society is spoiled, if pains are taken, if the associates are brought a mile to meet. And if it be not society, it is a mischievous, low, degrading jangle, though made up of the best. All the greatness of each is kept back, and every foible in painful activity, as if the Olympians should meet to exchange snuff-boxes.

Life goes headlong. We chase some flying scheme, or we are hunted by some fear or command behind us. But if suddenly we encounter a friend, we pause; our heat and hurry look foolish enough; now pause, now possession, is required, and the power to swell the moment from the resources of the heart. The moment is all, in all noble relations.

A divine person is the prophecy of the mind;

a friend is the hope of the heart. Our beati- How the grandeur of character acts tude waits for the fulfilment of these two in one. The ages are opening this moral force. All force is the shadow or symbol of that. Poetry is joyful and strong, as it draws its inspirations thence. Men write their names on the world, as they are filled with this. History has been mean ; our nations have been mobs ; we have never seen a man : that divine form we do not yet know, but only the dream and prophecy of such ; we do not know the majestic manners which belong to him, which appease and exalt the beholder. We shall one day see that the most private is the most public energy, that quality atones for quantity, and grandeur of character acts in the dark, and succours them who never saw it. What greatness has yet appeared, is beginnings and encouragements to us in this direction. The history of those gods and saints which the world has written, and then worshipped, are documents of character. The ages have exulted in the manners of a youth who owed nothing to fortune, and who was hanged at the Tyburn of his nation, who, by the pure quality of his nature, shed an epic splendour around the facts of his death, who has transfigured every particular into a universal symbol for the eyes of mankind. This great defeat is hitherto our highest fact. But the mind requires a victory to the senses, a force of character which will convert judge, jury, soldier, and king; which will rule animal and mineral virtues, and blend with the courses of sap, of rivers, of winds, of stars, and of mortal agents.

If we cannot attain at a bound to these grandeurs, at least let us do them homage. In society, high advantages are set down to the possessor as disadvantages. It requires the more wariness in our private estimates. I do not forgive in my friends the failure to know a fine character, and to entertain it with thankful hospitality. When, at last, that which we have always longed for, is arrived, and shines on us with glad rays, out of that far celestial land, then to be coarse, then to be critical, and treat such a visitant with the jabber and suspicion of the streets, argues a vulgarity that seems to shut the doors of heaven. This is confusion, this the right insanity, when the soul no longer knows its own, nor where its allegiance, its religion, are due. Is there any religion but this, to know, that, wherever in the wide desert of being, the holy sentiment we cherish has opened into a flower, it blooms for me? if none

72

sees it, I see it; I am aware, if I alone, of the
greatness of the fact. Whilst it blooms, I will
keep sabbath or holy time, and suspend my
gloom, and my folly and jokes. Nature is in-
dulged by the presence of this guest. There
are many eyes that can detect and honour the
prudent and household virtues; there are many
that can discern Genius on his starry track,
though the mob is incapable: but when that
love which is all-suffering, all-abstaining, all-
aspiring, which has vowed to itself, that it
will be a wretch, and also a fool in this world,
sooner than soil its white hands by any com-
pliances, comes into our streets and houses,—
only the pure and aspiring can know
its face, and the only compliment
they can pay it, is to own it.

COMPENSATION

EVER SINCE I WAS a boy, I have wished to write a discourse on Compensation: for it seemed to me when very young, that, on this subject, Life was ahead of theology, and the people knew more than the preachers taught. The documents, too, from which the doctrine is to be drawn, charmed my fancy by their endless variety, and lay always before me, even in sleep; for they are the tools in our hands, the bread in our basket, the transactions of the street, the farm, and the dwelling-house, the greetings, the relations, the debts and credits, the influence of character, the nature and endowment of all men. It seemed to me also that in it might be shown men a ray of divinity, the present action of the Soul of this world, clean from all vestige of tradition, and so the heart of man might be bathed by an inundation of eternal love, conversing with that which he knows was always and always must be, because it really is now. It appeared, moreover, that if this doctrine could be stated in terms with any resemblance to those bright intuitions in which this truth is sometimes revealed to us, it would be a star in many dark hours and crooked passages in our journey, that would not suffer us to lose our way.

I was lately confirmed in these desires by hearing a sermon at church. The preacher, a man esteemed for his orthodoxy, unfolded in the ordinary manner the doctrine of the Last Judgment. He assumed that judgment is not executed in this world; that the wicked are successful; that the good are miserable; and then urged from reason and from Scripture a compensation to be made to both parties in the next life. No offence appeared to be taken by the congregation at this doctrine. As far as I could observe, when the meeting broke up, they separated without remark on the sermon.

Yet what was the import of this teaching? What did the preacher mean by saying that the good are miserable in the present life? Was it that houses and lands, offices, wine, horses, dress, luxury, are had by unprincipled men, whilst the saints are poor and despised; and that a compensation is to be made to these last hereafter, by giving them the like gratifications another day, — bank-stock and doubloons, venison and champagne? This must be the compensation intended; for what else? Is it that they are to have leave to pray and praise? to love and serve men? Why, that they can do now. The legitimate inference the disciple would draw, was: 'We are to have such a good time as the sinners have now ';—or, to push it to its extreme import: 'You sin now; we shall sin by and by: we would sin now, if we could; not being successful, we expect our revenge to-morrow.'

The fallacy lay in the immense concession that the bad are successful; that justice is not done now. The blindness of the preacher consisted in deferring to the base estimate of the market of what constitutes a manly success, instead of confronting and convicting the world from the truth; announcing the Presence of the Soul, the omnipotence of the Will; and so establishing the standard of good and ill, of success and falsehood, and summoning the dead to its present tribunal.

I find a similar base tone in the popular religious works of the day, and the same doctrines assumed by the literary men when occasionally they treat the related topics. I think that our popular theology has gained in decorum, and not in principle, over the superstitions it has displaced. But men are better than this theology. Their daily life gives it the lie. Every ingenious and aspiring soul leaves the doctrine behind him in his own experience; and all men

79

feel sometimes the falsehood which they cannot demonstrate. For men are wiser than they
know. That which they hear in schools and
pulpits without afterthought, if said in conversation would probably be questioned in silence.
If a man dogmatise in a mixed company on
Providence and the divine laws, he is answered
by a silence which conveys well enough to an
observer the dissatisfaction of the hearer, but
his incapacity to make his own statement.

I shall attempt in this and the following
chapter to record some facts that indicate the
path of the law of Compensation; happy beyond my expectation, if I shall truly draw the
smallest arc of this circle.

POLARITY, or action and reaction, we meet
in every part of nature; in darkness and light;
in heat and cold; in the ebb and flow of waters;
in male and female; in the inspiration and ex-
piration of plants and animals; in the systole
and diastole of the heart; in the undulations
of fluid and of sound; in the centrifugal and
centripetal gravity; in electricity, galvanism,
and chemical affinity. Superinduce magnetism
at one end of a needle, the opposite magnetism
takes place at the other end. If the south at-
tracts, the north repels. To empty here, you

must condense there. An inevitable dualism bisects nature, so that each thing is a half, and suggests another thing to make it whole; as spirit, matter; man, woman; subjective, objective; in, out; upper, under; motion, rest; yea, nay.

Whilst the world is thus dual, so is every one of its parts. The entire system of things gets represented in every particle. There is somewhat that resembles the ebb and flow of the sea, day and night, man and woman, in a single needle of the pine, in a kernel of corn, in each individual of every animal tribe. The reaction so grand in the elements is repeated within these small boundaries. For example, in the animal kingdom, the physiologist has observed that no creatures are favourites, but a certain compensation balances every gift and every defect. A surplusage given to one part is paid out of a reduction from another part of the same creature. If the head and neck are enlarged, the trunk and extremities are cut short.

The theory of the mechanic forces is another example. What we gain in power is lost in time; and the converse. The periodic or compensating errors of the planets is another instance. The influences of climate and soil in political history are another. The cold climate invigorates; the barren soil does not breed fevers, crocodiles, tigers, or scorpions.

The same dualism underlies the nature and condition of man. Every excess causes a defect; every defect an excess. Every sweet hath its sour; every evil its good. Every faculty which is a receiver of pleasure, has an equal penalty put on its abuse. It is to answer for its moderation with its life. For every grain of wit there is a grain of folly. For everything you have missed, you have gained something else; and for everything you gain, you lose something. If riches increase, they are increased that use them. If the gatherer gathers too much, nature takes out of the man what she puts into his chest; swells the estate, but kills the owner. Nature hates monopolies and exceptions. The waves of the sea do not more speedily seek a level from their loftiest tossing, than the varieties of condition tend to equalise themselves. There is always some levelling circumstance, that puts down the overbearing, the strong, the rich, the fortunate, substantially on the same ground with all others. Is a man too strong and fierce for society, and by temper and position a bad citizen,—a morose ruffian with a dash of the pirate in him;— nature sends him a troop of pretty sons and daughters, who are getting along in the dame's classes at the village-school, and love and fear for them smooths his grim scowl to courtesy. Thus she contrives to intenerate the granite and felspar, takes the boar out and puts the lamb in, and keeps her balance true.

The farmer imagines power and place are fine things. But the President has paid dear for his White House. It has commonly cost him all his peace and the best of his manly attributes. To preserve for a short time so conspicuous an appearance before the world, he is content to eat dust before the real masters, who stand erect behind the throne. Or, do men desire the more substantial and permanent grandeur of genius? Neither has this an immunity. He who by force of will or of thought is great, and overlooks thousands, has the responsibility of overlooking. With every influx of light comes new danger. Has he light? he must bear witness to the light, and always outrun that sympathy which gives him such keen satisfaction, by his fidelity to new revelations of the incessant soul. He must hate father and mother, wife and child. Has he all that the world loves and admires and covets? he must cast behind him their admiration, and afflict them by faithfulness to his truth, and become a by-word and a hissing.

This Law writes the laws of cities and nations. It will not be baulked of its end in the smallest iota. It is in vain to build or plot or combine against it. Things refuse to be mismanaged long. Res nolunt diu male administrari. Though no checks to a new evil appear, the checks exist, and will appear. If the government is cruel, the governor's life is not safe. If you tax too high, the revenue will yield nothing. If you make the criminal code sanguinary, juries will not convict. Nothing arbitrary, nothing artificial can endure. The true life and satisfactions of man seem to elude the utmost rigours or felicities of condition, and to establish themselves with great indifferency under all varieties of circumstance. Under all governments the influence of character remains the same,—in Turkey and in New England about alike. Under the primeval despots of Egypt, history honestly confesses that man must have been as free as culture could make him.

These appearances indicate the fact that the universe is represented in every one of its particles. Everything in nature contains all the powers of nature. Everything is made of one hidden stuff; as the naturalist sees one Nothing artificial can endure type under every metamorphosis, and regards a horse as a running man, a fish as a swimming man, a bird as a flying man, a tree as a rooted man. Each new form repeats not only the main character of the type, but part for part all the details, all the aims, furtherances, hinderances, energies, and whole system of every other. Every occupation, trade, art, transaction, is a compend of the world, and a correlative of every other. Each one is an entire emblem of human life; of its good and ill, its trials, its enemies, its course, and its end. And each one must somehow accommodate the whole man, and recite all his destiny.

The world globes itself in a drop of dew. The microscope cannot find the animalcule which is less perfect for being little. Eyes, ears, taste, smell, motion, resistance, appetite, and organs of reproduction that take hold on eternity,—all find room to consist in the small creature. So do we put our life into every act. The true doctrine of omnipresence is, that God reappears with all his parts in every moss and cobweb. The value of the universe contrives to throw itself into every point. If the good is there, so is the evil; if the affinity, so the repulsion; if the force, so the limitation.

Thus is the universe alive. All things are
moral. That soul which within us is a sentiment, outside of us is a law. We feel its inspirations; out there in history we can see its
fatal strength. It is almighty. All nature feels
its grasp. 'It is in the world, and the world
was made by it.' It is eternal, but it enacts
itself in time and space. Justice is not post-
poned. A perfect equity adjusts its balance in
all parts of life. Οἱ κύβοι Διὸς ἀεὶ εὖ πίπτουσιν.
The dice of God are always loaded. The world
looks like a multiplication-table or a mathe-
matical equation, which, turn it how you will,
balances itself. Take what figure you will,
its exact value, nor more nor less, still returns
to you. Every secret is told, every crime is
punished, every virtue rewarded, every wrong
redressed, in silence and certainty. What we
call retribution is the universal necessity by
which the whole appears wherever a part appears. If you see smoke, there must be a fire.
If you see a hand or a limb, you know that the
trunk to which it belongs is there behind.

Every act rewards itself, or, in other words,
integrates itself, in a twofold manner; first, in
the thing, or in real nature; and secondly, in
the circumstance, or in apparent nature. Men
call the circumstance the retribution. The

causal retribution is in the thing, and is seen by the soul. The retribution in the circumstance is seen by the understanding; it is in-
separable from the thing, but is often spread
over a long time, and so does not become dis-
tinct until after many years. The specific
stripes may follow late after the offence, but
they follow because they accompany it. Crime
and punishment grow out of one stem. Punishment is a fruit that unsuspected ripens within
the flower of the pleasure which concealed it.
Cause and effect, means and ends, seed and
fruit, cannot be severed; for the effect already
blooms in the cause, the end pre-exists in the
means, the fruit in the seed.

Whilst thus the world will be whole, and
refuses to be disparted, we seek to act partially,
to sunder, to appropriate; for example,—to
gratify the senses, we sever the pleasure of the
senses from the needs of the character. The
ingenuity of man has been dedicated always to
the solution of one problem,—how to detach
the sensual sweet, the sensual strong, the
sensual bright, etc., from the moral sweet, the
moral deep, the moral fair; that is, again, to
contrive to cut clean off this upper surface so
thin as to leave it bottomless; to get a one
end, without an other end. The soul says, Eat;

the body would feast. The soul says, The man and woman shall be one flesh and one soul; the body would join the flesh only. The soul says, Have dominion over all things to the ends of virtue; the body would have the power over things to its own ends.

The soul strives amain to live and work through all things. It would be the only fact. All things shall be added unto it,—power, pleasure, knowledge, beauty. The particular man aims to be somebody; to set up for himself; to truck and higgle for a private good; and, in particulars, to ride, that he may ride; to dress, that he may be dressed; to eat, that he may eat; and to govern, that he may be seen. Men seek to be great; they would have offices, wealth, power, and fame. They think that to be great is to get only one side of nature—the sweet, without the other side—the bitter.

Steadily is this dividing and detaching counteracted. Up to this day, it must be owned, no projector has had the smallest success. The parted water reunites behind our hand. Pleasure is taken out of pleasant things, profit out of profitable things, power out of strong things, the moment we seek to separate them from the whole. We can no more halve things, and get the sensual good by itself, than we can get an inside that shall have no outside, or a light without a shadow. 'Drive out nature with a fork, she comes running back.'

Life invests itself with inevitable conditions, which the unwise seek to dodge, which one and another brags that he does not know; brags that they do not touch him;—but the brag is on his lips, the conditions are in his soul. If he escapes them in one part, they attack him in another more vital part. If he has escaped them in form and in the appearance, it is that he has resisted his life and fled from himself; and the retribution is so much death. So signal is the failure of all attempts to make this separation of the good from the tax, that the experiment would not be tried, —since to try it is to be mad,—but for the circumstance, that when the disease begins in the will, of rebellion and separation, the intellect is at once infected, so that the man ceases to see God whole in each object, but is able to see the sensual allurement of an object, and not see the sensual hurt; he sees the mermaid's head, but not the dragon's tail; and thinks he can cut off that which he would have, from that which he would not have. 'How secret art thou who dwellest in the highest heavens in silence, O thou only great God,

The human
soul is true
to these facts sprinkling with an unwearied Providence certain penal blindnesses upon such as have un-
bridled desires!'

The human soul is true to these facts in the
painting of fable, of history, of law, of proverbs, of conversation. It finds a tongue in
literature unawares. Thus the Greeks called
Jupiter, Supreme Mind; but having tradition-
ally ascribed to him many base actions, they
involuntarily made amends to Reason, by tying
up the hands of so bad a god. He is made as
helpless as a king of England. Prometheus
knows one secret, which Jove must bargain
for; Minerva, another. He cannot get his own
thunders; Minerva keeps the key of them.
' Of all the gods I only know the keys
   That ope the solid doors within whose vaults
   His thunders sleep.'
A plain confession of the in-working of the
All, and of its moral aim. The Indian my-
thology ends in the same ethics; and indeed
it would seem impossible for any fable to be
invented and get any currency which was not
moral. Aurora forgot to ask youth for her
lover, and so though Tithonus is immortal,
he is old. Achilles is not quite invulnerable;
for Thetis held him by the heel when she
dipped him in the Styx, and the sacred waters

did not wash that part. Siegfried, in the Nibelungen, is not quite immortal, for a leaf fell on his back whilst he was bathing in the Dragon's blood, and that spot which it covered is mortal. And so it always is. There is a crack in everything God has made. Always, it would seem, there is this vindictive circumstance stealing in at unawares, even into the wild poesy in which the human fancy attempted to make bold holyday, and to shake itself free of the old laws,—this backstroke, this kick of the gun, certifying that the law is fatal; that in Nature nothing can be given, all things are sold.

This is that ancient doctrine of Nemesis, who keeps watch in the Universe, and lets no offence go unchastised. The Furies, they said, are attendants on Justice, and if the sun in heaven should transgress his path, they would punish him. The poets related that stone walls, and iron swords, and leathern thongs, had an occult sympathy with the wrongs of their owners; that the belt which Ajax gave Hector dragged the Trojan hero over the field at the wheels of the car of Achilles; and the sword which Hector gave Ajax was that on whose point Ajax fell. They recorded, that when the Thasians erected a statue to Theogenes, a victor in the games, one of his rivals went to it by night, and endeavoured to throw it down by repeated blows, until at last he moved it from its pedestal, and was crushed to death beneath its fall.

This voice of fable has in it somewhat divine. It came from the thought above the will of the writer. That is the best part of each writer which has nothing private in it. That is the best part of each which he does not know, that which flowed out of his constitution, and not from his too active invention; that which in the study of a single artist you might not easily find, but in the study of many you would abstract as the spirit of them all. Phidias it is not, but the work of man in that early Hellenic world, that I would know. The name and circumstance of Phidias, however convenient for history, embarrasses when we come to the highest criticism. We are to see that which man was tending to do in a given period, and was hindered, or, if you will, modified in doing, by the interfering volitions of Phidias, of Dante, of Shakespeare, the organ whereby man at the moment wrought.

Still more striking is the expression of this fact in the proverbs of all nations, which are always the literature of Reason, or the state-

ments of an absolute truth without qualifica-
tion. Proverbs, like the sacred books of each
nation, are the sanctuary of the Intuitions.
That which the droning world, chained to
appearances, will not allow the realist to say
in his own words, it will suffer him to say in
proverbs without contradiction. And this law
of laws, which the pulpit, the senate, and the
college deny, is hourly preached in all markets
and all languages by flights of proverbs, whose
teaching is as true and as omnipresent as that
of birds and flies.

All things are double, one against another.
—Tit for tat; an eye for an eye; a tooth for
a tooth; blood for blood; measure for measure; love for love.—Give, and it shall be
given you.—He that watereth shall be watered
himself.—What will you have? quoth God;
pay for it, and take it.—Nothing venture, nothing have.—Thou shalt be paid exactly for
what thou hast done, no more, no less.—Who
doth not work shall not eat.—Harm watch,
harm catch.—Curses always recoil on the head
of him who imprecates them.—If you put a
chain around the neck of a slave, the other
end fastens itself around your own.—Bad
counsel confounds the adviser.—The devil is
an ass.

It is thus written, because it is thus in life. Our action is overmastered and characterised above our will by the law of nature. We aim at a petty end, quite aside from the public good, but our act arranges itself by irresistible magnetism in a line with the poles of the world.

A man cannot speak but he judges himself. With his will, or against his will, he draws his portrait to the eye of his companions by every word. Every opinion reacts on him who utters it. It is a threadball thrown at a mark, but the other end remains in the thrower's bag. Or rather, it is a harpoon thrown at the whale, unwinding, as it flies, a coil of cord in the boat; and if the harpoon is not good, or not well thrown, it will go nigh to cut the steersman in twain, or to sink the boat.

You cannot do wrong without suffering wrong. ' No man had ever a point of pride that was not injurious to him,' said Burke. The exclusive in fashionable life does not see that he excludes himself from enjoyment, in the attempt to appropriate it. The exclusionist in religion does not see that he shuts the door of heaven on himself, in striving to shut out others. Treat men as pawns and ninepins, and you shall suffer as well as they. If you leave out their heart, you shall lose your own. The senses would make things of all persons; of women, of children, of the poor. The vulgar proverb, ' I will get it from his purse or get it from his skin,' is sound philosophy.

All infractions of love and equity in our social relations are speedily punished. They are punished by Fear. Whilst I stand in simple relations to my fellow man, I have no displeasure in meeting him. We meet as water meets water, or a current of air meets another, with perfect diffusion and interpenetration of nature. But as soon as there is any departure from simplicity and attempt at halfness, or good for me that is not good for him, my neighbour feels the wrong; he shrinks from me as far as I have shrunk from him; his eyes no longer seek mine; there is war between us; there is hate in him, and fear in me.

All the old abuses in society, the great and universal, and the petty and particular, all unjust accumulations of property and power, are avenged in the same manner. Fear is an instructor of great sagacity, and the herald of all revolutions. One thing he always teaches, that there is rottenness where he appears. He is a carrion crow; and though you see not well what he hovers for, there is death somewhere. Our property is timid, our laws are timid, our cultivated classes are timid. Fear for ages has boded and mowed and gibbered over government and property. That obscene bird is not there for nothing. He indicates great wrongs, which must be revised.

Of the like nature is that expectation of change which instantly follows the suspension of our voluntary activity. The terror of cloudless moon, the emerald of Polycrates, the awe of prosperity, the instinct which leads every generous soul to impose on itself tasks of a noble asceticism and vicarious virtue, are the tremblings of the balance of justice through the heart and mind of man.

Experienced men of the world know very well that it is always best to pay scot and lot as they go along, and that a man often pays dear for a small frugality. The borrower runs in his own debt. Has a man gained anything who has received a hundred favours and rendered none? Has he gained by borrowing, through indolence or cunning, his neighbour's wares, or horses, or money? There arises on the deed the instant acknowledgment of benefit on the one part, and of debt on the other; that is, of superiority and inferiority. The transaction remains in the memory of himself

and his neighbour; and every new transaction
alters, according to its nature, their relation to
each other. He may soon come to see that
he had better have broken his own bones than
to have ridden in his neighbour's coach, and
that ' the highest price he can pay for a thing
is to ask for it.'

A wise man will extend this lesson to all
parts of life, and know that it is always the part
of prudence to face every claimant, and pay
every just demand on your time, your talents,
or your heart. Always pay; for, first or last,
you must pay your entire debt. Persons and
events may stand for a time between you and
justice, but it is only a postponement. You
must pay at last your own debt. If you are
wise, you will dread a prosperity which only
loads you with more. Benefit is the end of
nature. But for every benefit which you receive, a tax is levied. He is great who confers
the most benefits. He is base,—and that is
the one base thing in the universe,—to receive
favours, and render none. In the order of
nature we cannot render benefits to those from
whom we receive them, or only seldom. But
the benefit we receive must be rendered again,
line for line, deed for deed, cent for cent, to
somebody. Beware of too much good staying

in your hand. It will fast corrupt and worm worms. Pay it away quickly in some sort.

Labour is watched over by the same pitiless laws. Cheapest, say the prudent, is the dearest labour. What we buy in a broom, a mat, a wagon, a knife is some application of good sense to a common want. It is best to pay in your land a skilful gardener, or to buy good sense applied to gardening; in your sailor, good sense applied to navigation; in the house, good sense applied to cooking, sewing, serving; in your agent, good sense applied to accounts and affairs. So do you multiply your presence, or spread yourself throughout your estate. But because of the dual constitution of all things, in labour as in life there can be no cheating. The thief steals from himself. The swindler swindles himself. For the real price of labour is knowledge and virtue, whereof wealth and credit are signs. These signs, like paper-money, may be counterfeited or stolen, but that which they represent, namely, knowledge and virtue, cannot be counterfeited or stolen. These ends of labour cannot be answered but by real exertions of the mind, and in obedience to pure motives. The cheat, the defaulter, the gambler, cannot extort the benefit, cannot extort the knowledge of material and moral nature, which his honest care and pains yield to the operative. The law of nature is, Do the thing, and you shall have the power : but they who do not the thing have not the power.

Human labour, through all its forms, from the sharpening of a stake to the construction of a city or an epic, is one immense illustration of the perfect compensation of the universe. Everywhere and always this law is sublime. The absolute balance of Give and Take, the doctrine that everything has its price; and if that price is not paid, not that thing, but something else, is obtained, and that it is impossible to get anything without its price,—this doctrine is not less sublime in the columns of a ledger than in the budgets of states, in the laws of light and darkness, in all the action and reaction of nature. I cannot doubt that the high laws which each man sees ever implicated in those processes with which he is conversant, the stern ethics which sparkle on his chisel-edge, which are measured out by his plumb and foot-rule, which stand as manifest in the footing of the shop-bill as in the history of a state,—do recommend to him his trade, and, though seldom named, exalt his business to his imagination.

The league between virtue and nature en-
gages all things to assume a hostile front to
vice. The beautiful laws and substances of
the world persecute and whip the traitor. He
finds that things are arranged for truth and
benefit, but there is no den in the wide world to
hide a rogue. There is no such thing as con-
cealment. Commit a crime, and the earth is
made of glass. Commit a crime, and it seems as
if a coat of snow fell on the ground, such as re-
veals in the woods the track of every partridge
and fox and squirrel and mole. You cannot
recall the spoken word, you cannot wipe out
the foot-track, you cannot draw up the ladder,
so as to leave no inlet or clue. Always some
damning circumstance transpires. The laws
and substances of nature, water, snow, wind,
gravitation, become penalties to the thief.

On the other hand, the law holds with equal
sureness for all right action. Love, and you
shall be loved. All love is mathematically just,
as much as the two sides of an algebraic equation. The good man has absolute good, which
like fire turns everything to its own nature, so
that you cannot do him any harm ; but as the
royal armies sent against Napoleon, when he
approached, cast down their colours, and from
enemies became friends, so do disasters, of all

kinds, as sickness, offence, poverty, prove benefactors.

    ' Winds blow and waters roll
    Strength to the brave, and power and deity,
    Yet in themselves are nothing.'

The good are befriended even by weakness and defect. As no man had ever a point of pride that was not injurious to him, so no man had ever a defect that was not somewhere made useful to him. The stag in the fable admired his horns and blamed his feet; but when the hunter came, his feet saved him, and afterwards, caught in the thicket, his horns destroyed him. Every man in his lifetime needs to thank his faults. As no man thoroughly understands a truth until first he has contended against it, so no man has a thorough acquaintance with the hindrances or talents of men, until he has suffered from the one, and seen the triumph of the other over his own want of the same. Has he a defect of temper that unfits him to live in society? Thereby he is driven to entertain himself alone, and acquire habits of self-help; and thus, like the wounded oyster, he mends his shell with pearl.

Our strength grows out of our weakness. Not until we are pricked and stung and sorely shot at, awakens the indignation which arms itself with secret forces. A great man is always willing to be little. Whilst he sits on the cushion of advantages, he goes to sleep. When he is pushed, tormented, defeated, he has a chance to learn something; he has been put on his wits, on his manhood; he has gained facts; learns his ignorance; is cured of the insanity of conceit; has got moderation and real skill. The wise man always throws himself on the side of his assailants. It is more his interest than it is theirs to find his weak point. The wound cicatrises and falls off from him, like a dead skin; and when they would triumph, lo! he has passed on invulnerable. Blame is safer than praise. I hate to be defended in a newspaper. As long as all that is said, is said against me, I feel a certain assurance of success. But as soon as honied words of praise are spoken for me, I feel as one that lies unprotected before his enemies. In general, every evil to which we do not succumb is a benefactor. As the Sandwich Islander believes that the strength and valour of the enemy he kills passes into himself, so we gain the strength of the temptation we resist.

The same guards which protect us from disaster, defect, and enmity, defend us, if we will, from selfishness and fraud. Bolts and bars are not the best of our institutions, nor is shrewd- Never cheated by any one but himself ness in trade a mark of wisdom. Men suffer all their life long under the foolish superstition that they can be cheated. But it is as impossible for a man to be cheated by any one but himself, as for a thing to be and not to be at the same time. There is a third silent party to all our bargains. The nature and soul of things takes on itself the guaranty of the fulfilment of every contract, so that honest service cannot come to loss. If you serve an ungrateful master, serve him the more. Put God in your debt. Every stroke shall be repaid. The longer the payment is withholden, the better for you; for compound interest on compound interest is the rate and usage of this exchequer.

The history of persecution is a history of endeavours to cheat nature, to make water run uphill, to twist a rope of sand. It makes no difference whether the actors be many or one, a tyrant or a mob. A mob is a society of bodies voluntarily bereaving themselves of reason and traversing its work. The mob is man voluntarily descending to the nature of the beast. Its fit hour of activity is night. Its actions are insane, like its whole constitution. It persecutes a principle; it would whip a right; it would tar-and-feather justice, by inflicting fire and outrage upon the houses and persons of those who have these. It resembles the prank of boys who run with fire-engines to put out the ruddy aurora streaming to the stars. The inviolate spirit turns their spite against the wrong-doers. The martyr cannot be dishonoured. Every lash inflicted is a tongue of fame; every prison a more illustrious abode; every burned book or house enlightens the world; every suppressed or expunged word reverberates through the earth from side to side. The minds of men are at last aroused; reason looks out and justifies her own, and malice finds all her work vain. It is the whipper who is whipped, and the tyrant who is undone.

Thus do all things preach the indifference of circumstances. The man is all. Everything has two sides, a good and an evil. Every advantage has its tax. I learn to be content. But the doctrine of compensation is not the doctrine of indifferency. The thoughtless say, on hearing these representations: What boots it to do well? there is one event to good and evil: if I gain any good, I must pay for it; if I lose any good, I gain some other; all actions are indifferent.

There is a deeper fact in the soul than compensation; to wit, its own nature. The soul is not a compensation, but a life. The soul is. Under all this running sea of circumstance, whose waters ebb and flow with perfect balance, lies the aboriginal abyss of real Being. Existence, or God, is not a relation, or a part, but the whole. Being is the vast affirmative, excluding negation, self-balanced, and swallowing up all relations, parts, and times, within itself. Nature, truth, virtue, are the influx from thence. Vice is the absence or departure of the same. Nothing, Falsehood, may indeed stand as the great Night or shade, on which, as a background, the living universe paints itself forth; but no fact is begotten by it; it cannot work; for it is not. It cannot work any good; it cannot work any harm. It is harm, inasmuch as it is worse not to be than to be.

We feel defrauded of the retribution due to evil acts, because the criminal adheres to his vice and contumacy, and does not come to a crisis or judgment anywhere in visible nature. There is no stunning confutation of his nonsense before men and angels. Has he therefore outwitted the law? Inasmuch as he carries the malignity and the lie with him, he so far deceases from nature. In some manner there will be a demonstration of the wrong to the understanding also; but should we not see it, this deadly deduction makes square the eternal account.

Neither can it be said, on the other hand, that the gain of rectitude must be bought by any loss. There is no penalty to virtue; no penalty to wisdom; they are proper additions of being. In a virtuous action, I properly am; in a virtuous act, I add to the world; I plant into deserts conquered from Chaos and Nothing, and see the darkness receding on the limits of the horizon. There can be no excess to love, none to knowledge, none to beauty, when these attributes are considered in the purest sense. The soul refuses all limits. It affirms in man always an Optimism, never a Pessimism.

His life is a progress, and not a station. His instinct is trust. Our instinct uses 'more' and 'less' in application to man, always of the presence of the soul, and not of its absence: the brave man is greater than the coward; the true, the benevolent, the wise, is more a man, and not less, than the fool and knave. There is, therefore, no tax on the good of virtue; for that is the incoming of God himself, or absolute existence, without any comparative. All external good has its tax; and if it came without The tax of gain is certain desert or sweat, has no root in me, and the next wind will blow it away. But all the good of nature is the soul's, and may be had, if paid for in nature's lawful coin, that is, by labour, which the heart and the head allow. I no longer wish to meet a good I do not earn—for example, to find a pot of buried gold—knowing that it brings with it new responsibility. I do not wish more external goods,—neither possessions, nor honours, nor powers, nor persons. The gain is apparent, the tax is certain. But there is no tax on the knowledge that the compensation exists, and that it is not desirable to dig up treasure. Herein I rejoice with a serene eternal peace. I contract the boundaries of possible mischief. I learn the wisdom of St. Bernard: 'Nothing can work me damage except myself; the harm that I sustain, I carry about with me, and never am a real sufferer but by my own fault.'

In the nature of the soul is the compensation for the inequalities of condition. The radical tragedy of nature seems to be the distinction of More and Less. How can Less not feel the pain; how not feel indignation or malevolence towards More? Look at those who have less faculty, and one feels sad, and

knows not well what to make of it. Almost
he shuns their eye; almost he fears they will
upbraid God. What should they do? It seems
a great injustice. But face the facts, and see
them nearly, and these mountainous inequalities vanish. Love reduces them all, as the sun
melts the iceberg in the sea. The heart and
soul of all men being one, this bitterness of
His and Mine ceases. His is mine. I am my
brother, and my brother is me. If I feel over-
shadowed and outdone by great neighbours,
I can yet love; I can still receive; and he that
loveth maketh his own the grandeur he loves.
Thereby I make the discovery that my brother
is my guardian, acting for me with the friend-
liest designs, and the estate I so admired and
envied is my own. It is the eternal nature of
the soul to appropriate and make all things
its own. Jesus and Shakespeare are fragments
of the soul, and by love I conquer and incor-
porate them in my own conscious domain. His
virtue,—is not that mine? His wit,—if it cannot be made mine, it is not wit.

Such, also, is the natural history of calamity.
The changes which break up at short intervals
the prosperity of men are advertisements of a
nature whose law is growth. Evermore it is
the order of nature to grow, and every soul is

by this intrinsic necessity quitting its whole According to the vigour of the individual system of things, its friends, and home, and laws, and faith, as the shell-fish crawls out of its beautiful but stony case, because it no longer admits of its growth, and slowly forms a new house. In proportion to the vigour of the individual, these revolutions are frequent, until in some happier mind they are incessant, and all worldly relations hang very loosely about him, becoming, as it were, a transparent fluid membrane through which the form is always seen, and not, as in most men, an indurated heterogeneous fabric of many dates, and of no settled character, in which the man is imprisoned. Then there can be enlargement, and the man of to-day scarcely recognises the man of yesterday. And such should be the outward biography of man in time,—a putting off of dead circumstances day by day, as he renews his raiment day by day. But to us, in our lapsed estate, resting not advancing, resisting not co-operating with the divine expansion, this growth comes by shocks.

We cannot part with our friends. We cannot let our angels go. We do not see that they only go out that archangels may come in. We are idolaters of the Old. We do not believe in the riches of the soul, in its proper eternity

and omnipresence. We do not believe there
is any force in to-day to rival or recreate that
beautiful yesterday. We linger in the ruins of
the old tent, where once we had bread and
shelter and organs, nor believe that the spirit
can feed, cover, and nerve us again. We cannot again find aught so dear, so sweet, so grace-
ful. But we sit and weep in vain. The voice
of the Almighty saith, ' Up and onward for
evermore!' We cannot stay amid the ruins.
Neither will we rely on the New: and so we
walk ever with reverted eyes, like those mon-
sters who look backwards.

And yet the compensations of calamity are
made apparent to the understanding also, after
long intervals of time. A fever, a mutilation,
a cruel disappointment, a loss of wealth, a loss
of friends, seems at the moment unpaid loss,
and unpayable. But the sure years reveal the
deep remedial force that underlies all facts.
The death of a dear friend, wife, brother, lover,
which seemed nothing but privation, somewhat
later assumes the aspect of a guide or genius;
for it commonly operates revolutions in our
way of life, terminates an epoch of infancy or
of youth which was waiting to be closed, breaks
up a wonted occupation, or a household, or
style of living, and allows the formation of new

ones more friendly to the growth of character.
It permits or constrains the formation of new
acquaintances, and the reception of new influences, that prove of the first importance to the
next years; and the man or woman who would
have remained a sunny garden-flower, with no
room for its roots, and too much sunshine for
its head, by the falling of the walls and the
neglect of the gardener, is made the banian of
the forest, yielding shade and fruit to
wide neighbourhoods of men.

www.ingramcontent.com/pod-product-compliance
Lightning Source LLC
Chambersburg PA
CBHW032235080426
42735CB00008B/872